Steal Away Home

By

AURAND HARRIS

A dramatization of the book
"Steal Away Home" 69-70
By Jane Kristof

Musical research and accompaniments
By Carolyn Geer

ROYALTY NOTE

The possession of this book, without a written authorization first having been obtained from the publisher, confers no right or license, to professionals or amateurs, to produce the play, publicly or in private, for gain or charity.

In its present form, this play is dedicated to the reading public only, and not to producers. However, productions of this play are encouraged, and those who wish to present it may secure the necessary permission by writing to The Anchorage Press, Cloverlot, Anchorage, Kentucky 40223, USA.

Professional producers are requested to apply to The Anchorage Press for royalty quotation.

This play may be presented by amateurs, upon payment to The Anchorage Press, of a royalty of $25.00 for each performance, one week before the date the play is to be given. The play is fully protected by copyright, and anyone presenting the play without the consent of The Anchorage Press, will be liable to the penalties provided by the copyright law.

Whenever the play is produced, the name of the author must be carried in all publicity, advertising, fliers, and programmes. Also the following notice must appear on all printed programmes: "Produced by special arrangement with The Anchorage Press, of Anchorage, Kentucky."

Steal Away Home

CAST:

(Since many in the cast appear in only one scene, the producer can use the same actor to play more than one role. Thus, by judicious doubling, the play can be cast with thirteen actors.)

PREACHER PRENTICE
AMOS, twelve years old
OBIE, ten years old
*MAN WITH GUN
MAMA
*MRS. STRAUSS
MISS MELISSA
*EDGAR
JOE
*FIRST MAN
*SECOND MAN
*ELIJAH McNAUL
*JUD
*FIRST NEIGHBOR
*SECOND NEIGHBOR
*OLD MAN
*YOUNG MAN
JACK
*PATROL
*WILL
*MOTHER
*CONDUCTOR
PA
*STAGEHANDS
CHOIR

(* Can be doubled.)

SCENE:

Stations on the Underground Railroad from South Carolina to Pennsylvania, 1854.

MUSIC CUES

For

Steal Away Home

Cue 1. "Didn't My Lord Deliver Daniel?"

Cue 2. "Didn't My Lord Deliver Daniel?"

Cue 3. "Sometimes I Feel Like a Motherless Child"

Cue 4. "Gonna Sing All Along the Way"

Cue 5. "Who Built the Ark?"

Cue 6. "The Old Ark's a-Moverin'"

Cue 7. "Steal Away"

Cue 8. "Oh, Rock-a My Soul"

Cue 9. "Gonna Sing All Along the Way"

Cue 10. "Go Down Moses"

Cue 11. "Heav'n-Bound Soldier"

Cue 12. "You'd Better Run", with Rhythms

Cue 13. "Steal Away"

Cue 14. "The Angel of the Lord"

Cue 15. "You'd Better Run", with Rhythms

Cue 16. "Jim Crack Corn"

Cue 17. "Oh, Rock-a My Soul"

Cue 18. "Git On Board"

Cue 19. "Train Song"

Cue 20. "Steal Away"

Cue 21. "Didn't My Lord Deliver Daniel?"

Complete piano score for the music required by this play is available at $10.00 per copy, from Anchorage Press, Inc., Cloverlot, Anchorage, Kentucky 40223.

The music cue numbers used in the play-book refer to this authorized score.

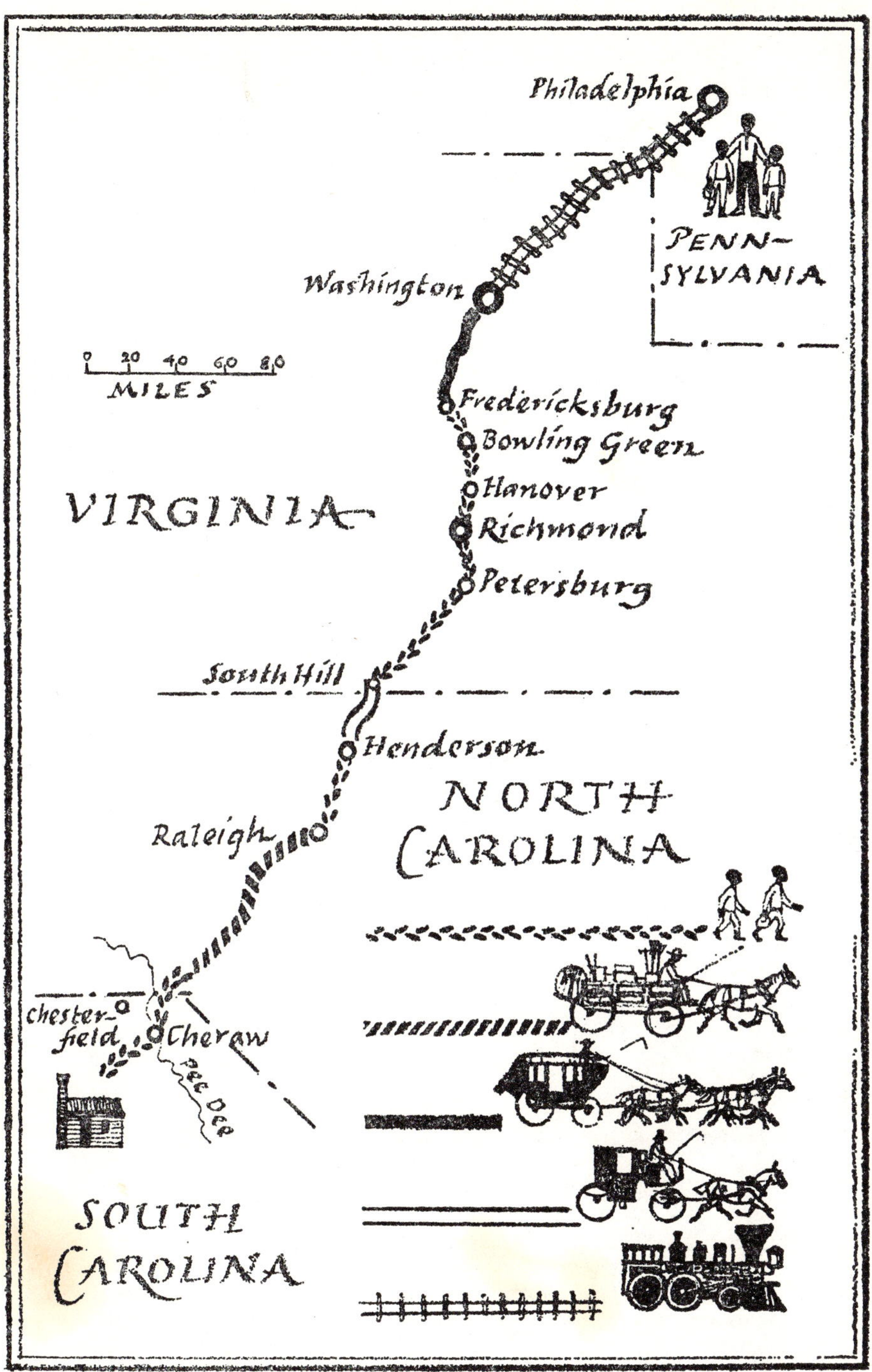

Illustration by W. T. Mars. Reprinted with permission from the book, "Steal Away Home" by Jane Kristof, Copyright 1969 by The Bobbs Merrill Company, Inc. Library of Congress Catalog Card No. 78-84168. All rights reserved.

The premiere production of *Steal Away Home* was given 13 February, 1972, by the Louisville Children's Theatre and the West Side Players, at Louisville, Kentucky. Following is a copy of the programme for this performance:

Louisville Children's Theatre and The West Side Players

Present The World Premiere of

Steal Away Home

by AURAND HARRIS

A dramatization of the book "Steal Away Home" by JANE KRISTOF— Music Research by CAROLYN GEER—Directed by BEKKI JO SCHNEIDER and CARROLL SCHEMPP—Set Design by HENRY THARP—Costume Design by MARGE SIMON—Musical Direction by STEVE PLANK (The Louisville Youth Choir) Musical Accompaniment by JANICE COSBY.

CAST

AMOS	Clifford Warfield
OBIE	Bryon Woods
PREACHER PRENTICE	Eugene Rodgers
MAMA	Mera Cole, Cecilia Blye
MAN WITH THE GUN	Don Adkins
MRS. STRAUSS	Barbara Taylor, Natalie West
MISS MELISSA	Debbie Schneider, Sandy Richens
EDGAR	Ed Jenkins, Ted Swanner
JOE	Ogen Buckner, Ron Elmore
FIRST MAN	Kevin Pawley
SECOND MAN	Chris Robare
ELIJAH McNAUL	Lou Bandy, Kevin Pawley
JUD	Larry Singer
FIRST NEIGHBOR	David Silverman
SECOND NEIGHBOR	Don Wibbels
OLD MAN	Don Adkins
FIRST YOUNG MAN	Dick Johnston
SECOND YOUNG MAN	David Lentendre
JACK	A. W. Dayton
PATROL	Don Wibbels
WILL	Alex Ward, Eric Friedlander
MOTHER	Barbara Cassin
CONDUCTOR	David Letendre
PA	Bill Lathon
STAGE-HANDS	Chris Robare, Robert Pickett, Ron Atik, Glen McElroy

Several roles are double-cast. The name listed first will play for opening performance.

CHORUS

Jackie Atkins	Donna McElroy	Regina Washington
Jerry Jackson	Deborah Leslie	Debbie White
Karyn Marshall	Janet Lomax	Elizabeth Dulan

The play takes place in 1853, along the Freedom Railroad, from South Carolina to Pennsylvania. There will be one intermission.

Steal Away Home

ACT ONE

(Choir sings softly. Cue 1. "Didn't My Lord Deliver Daniel?" The curtains open on a bare stage. Amos, twelve years old and a slave, enters right, singing with the choir the last of the hymn with great enjoyment).

AMOS. ". . . Didn't my Lord deliver Daniel, deliver Daniel, deliver Daniel, Didn't my Lord deliver Daniel, and why not-a every man?"

(He looks at the audience and smiles).

That's my favorite song. We sang it the Sunday when Preacher Prentice came to the plantation—that Sunday when it all began.

(Comes to footlights and speaks intimately).

Preacher Prentice was born a slave, like me; but his master freed him. He could read and write and he had a cart and a horse and traveled around fixing pots and pans. The white folks called him a tinker, but to us he was the Preacher. Well, that Sunday Obie and me sat right up close to hear him preach. After the meeting and all the singing, Obie and me walked home, kicking our feet in the dust like always—never thinking—never knowing that— that day—that Sunday, May 29, 1854—that that was the day our big adventure was going to begin.

(He steps into the scene).

I was almost to our cabin and I could smell supper cooking and I could smell Mama's honeysuckle blooming on the gate.

(A weathered, dilapidated gate is placed at left by stagehands).

And Obie was dawdling behind, seeing how far he could jump on one foot.

(Calls off right).

Obie. Come on, Obie. I'll race you to the cabin. Obie! Mama's waiting supper for us. OBIE!! I smell—benne cakes!

OBIE *(Age ten, talkative and lively, runs in at right and dashes across the stage through gate, exiting at left, shouting).* Benne cakes! Come on! I'm hungry!

AMOS. Wait for me.

PREACHER *(Preacher Prentice enters right).* Just a minute, young fellow.

AMOS. Preacher Prentice!

PREACHER. I saw you at the meeting, didn't I?

(Amos nods).

You and your brother?

(Amos nods).

Your Pa—his name is Henry?

AMOS. Yes, sir. He belonged to Master Smithers but they took Pa with them when they moved away five years ago.

PREACHER *(Nods).* Is your Mama in the cabin?

AMOS. Yes, sir.

MAMA *(Quickly enters from left, coming through gate. Obie follows close behind).* I'm right here, Preacher Prentice.

PREACHER. You the wife of Henry that belonged to the Smithers?

MAMA. That's right. But when they moved away from South Carolina they took Henry with them.

PREACHER *(Speaks in secret).* I have something—for you.

(He looks around).

Nobody's around, are they?

(All look. Preacher speaks in a hushed voice).

Don't want nobody to see me or nobody to hear what I got to say.

MAMA *(Fearful).* Nobody here but us.

PREACHER *(Carefully takes a folded piece of paper from inside band of his hat. Speaks cautiously).* I got a letter for you—from Henry.

MAMA. A letter?

PREACHER *(Carefully so no one will see, hands letter to Mama).* He sent it by me.

MAMA. A letter from Henry!

PREACHER. Sh! Someone will hear you.

MAMA *(Holds out letter).* I can't read.

PREACHER *(Reads slowly and confidentially).* "My dear wife. Master Smithers took sick and died, but he set me free. I went north—"

MAMA. Free! Your Pa's free!

PREACHER *(Looks around fearfully).* Hush. "I took the name of Carpenter and live in a town called Lemhorn near the city of Philadelphia. I work and save and hope I'll have enough money to buy you and little Sally from Master Bricker.

(Reads with emphasis).

I wish Amos and Obadiah were here to help me. God bless and keep you all. Your loving husband."

Mama. He's going to buy little Sally and me. We'll be free with him.

Obie. What about us, Mama? He didn't say nothing about buying Amos and me. Don't Pa want us?

Amos. 'Course Pa wants us, but—but he don't have enough money to buy all four. Mama's first. And little Sally, she's so sickly I expect Master will sell her cheap.

Obie (*Beams with a comforting idea*). Maybe he wants us—you and me—Amos, wants us—to run off! Go north and help him!

Mama. Don't talk foolish.

Preacher (*Slowly and pointedly*). Maybe—that's just what he do want.

(*All look at him in surprise, Obie more surprised than the others*).

Mama. What do you mean?

Preacher (*Looks around cautiously, then speaks with excitement*). He wrote those words big. "I wish Amos and Obediah were here to help me." It's got to mean something special.

Mama (*Fearful*). You think he wants them to run away—go up north! They're just children.

Preacher. There'd be folks that would help them along the road.

Mama. Folks?

Preacher. Folks on the underground railroad.

Amos. The what?

Preacher. The underground railroad.

Obie. What's that?

Preacher. It's people. People who help runaway slaves. They hide you and then send you on to the next station—and to the next and to the next—until at last you're safe and free. I figure the two of you could do it.

Amos. Us?

Obie. How?

Preacher (*All listen carefully as Preacher speaks in hushed voice but with excitement*). Master Bricker will give you a day off on the Fourth of July.

(*All nod*).

That comes on a Monday. Now if you'd steal away Sunday morning *early,* you'd have two days start before he knowed you was gone.

(*Boys nod*).

You could slip along to the new bridge over the Pee Dee River and hide there, till I come along in my cart. Then in you'd crawl and I'd start you north on the underground railroad.

AMOS. What about Mama? If we run away, Master will blame her.

MAMA. If my boys were free, there wouldn't be nothing Master could do would hurt me.

(Hugs boys).

PREACHER. He'd never know if you runned off, or if you got stolen, or got drowned, or what.

OBIE. Can we go, Mama?

MAMA. It's so far.

PREACHER *(Nods).* It's five hundred miles to Philadelphia.

MAMA. You're so little.

PREACHER. You think about it, and you'll decide the right way.

(Looks about to see if anyone is watching).

Goodby. I've got a feeling I'll see you boys again—hiding under the bridge, ready to ride to freedom.

(He exits right).

AMOS *(Whispers excitedly).* Can we go, Mama? Can we go?

MAMA. I don't know what to say. If your Pa wants you—

OBIE. Can we, Mama?

MAMA. Five hundred miles—

AMOS AND OBIE. Can we? Can we?

MAMA *(Looks at them, off after Preacher, then nods her head).* Yes. I can't stop you from going free.

OBIE *(Bounces with excitement and shouts with joy).* We're going! We're going!

MAMA. Hush, Obie. Quick—get inside the cabin.

(Fearful, she motions him toward cabin. Obie exits through gate, off left).

You're going north. You're going to your Pa.

(Embraces Amos).

It's a long way. They'll try to stop you—try to catch you, but I'm trusting in you, Amos. And I'm trusting in the good Lord.

(She exits through gate and off left).

(Amos radiant, sings the words of the song with true conviction. Choir joins him. Cue 2. "Didn't My Lord Deliver Daniel?")

(Amos exits through gate and off left. The singing continues as lights dim down slightly. The singing becomes a hum as lights come up slowly. It is sun-up and Mama enters cautiously from left. She enters through gate, then beckons boys who enter left, carrying short fishing poles. Singing stops).

MAMA *(She is nervous and tries to keep back her tears. She speaks cautiously).* It's time to go—before anybody's up.

(She looks about fearfully).

You remember all I told you?

(Boys nod).

Cut through the woods to the stream. Keep wading in the water so you'll leave no tracks if Master sets the hounds to find you. Follow the creek till it runs into the Pee Dee River. That won't be till tomorrow. Then hide—don't let nobody see you! Hide under the new bridge and wait.

AMOS *(Not as brave as he sounds).* We will, Mama.

(Frightened).

Come on, Obie. It's getting light.

OBIE *(Afraid now that it is happening).* How far is it to—

(Has a comic difficulty pronouncing it).

Phil—A—delph'a?

MAMA. Preacher said five hundred miles.

OBIE *(Starts to cry).* I'm going to miss you, Mama.

MAMA *(Trying not to cry, gives him small sack).* Here, take your sack. Some turnips and benne cakes.

OBIE *(Crying).* I ain't hungry.

MAMA. You will be.

(Nervous and fearful).

Now—hurry before someone sees you.

OBIE *(Sobbing, embraces Mama).* Goodby, Mama.

MAMA *(Crying, kisses him).* Goodby. You mustn't cry.

(Bravely, overcoming her crying).

Remember—keep remembering you're going to your Pa—you're going to be free.

AMOS *(Crying).* We will, Mama. Goodby.

(Embraces her).

Goodby, Mama.

MAMA. Goodby.

(*Kisses him, crying*).

Take care. Take care of Obie. Take care of yourself.

AMOS (*Crying freely*). I will, Mama. Come on, Obie.

(*Takes his hand and the two boys start right, both crying and rubbing their noses*).

Don't cry. Hold your head up. Keep saying—we're going to be free—free—

(*They exit right*).

MAMA. I can't do no more for them, Lord. They're in your hands. Help them find the way.

(*Humming begins as she exits left. Cue 3. "Sometimes I Feel Like A Motherless Child." Gate is removed. Humming continues. Lights come up bright. Amos and Obie enter right, walking wearily. Singing fades out*).

OBIE. I could eat some benne cakes.

AMOS. Me, too.

(*They sit downstage, eat and talk with their mouths full*).

OBIE. Yesterday when we left I didn't think I could ever eat again. My feet feel like they'd walked forever. But I guess your feet hurt more.

AMOS. Why?

OBIE. Cause your feet are bigger.

(*Wiggles his toes*).

I keep thinking of Mama. What you reckon she's doing?

AMOS. Praying that we'll be safe.

OBIE. What you reckon Pa is doing?

AMOS. Pa?

(*A new realization*).

You know, Obie—we won't even know Pa.

OBIE. But he'll know us! And when we get there we'll help him work so he can buy Mama and Sally.

AMOS. And we'll have a little house—on a little farm—

OBIE. And you know what else? A little puppy.

AMOS. Remember when Master lost his puppy? He searched two days for that dog. I know he liked that dog better than he liked us, but we're worth more money.

(Fearful).

I reckon he'll hunt harder to find us.

OBIE *(Also afraid).* Amos, what'll they do if they catch us?

(There is a sudden sharp sound off-stage. Obie jumps up alarmed).

What's that! What's that, Amos?

AMOS. Hush!

(They crouch, frozen with fear. Amos slowly looks around. He whispers).

Come on. Come on, Obie. We have to keep going.

(Fearful, they start left).

Let's see what's around the bend in the river. Come on!

(They run a few steps, stop, and Amos points down left with joy).

Look! There's a bridge.

OBIE. It's a new bridge!

AMOS. It's the one he said! We'll hide under it and wait until he comes.

OBIE *(Frightened).* Amos, what if he doesn't come?

AMOS. He said he would—and *he's* a preacher!

OBIE *(Suddenly joyful with relief).* Amen! Sing hallelujah.

*(Choir sings. Cue 4. "Gonna Sing All Along The Way." Obie dances off left after Amos who motions for him to hurry.
A horse and cart move on stage at right. It is a side view of a horse hitched to a cart, a one dimensional cut-out painted front. The cart is backed by a practical platform on which are pots, pans, barrels, etc. Preacher Prentice sits on the driver's seat, driving the horse and slapping the reins).*

PREACHER. Whoa! Whoa there!

(Horse and cart stop at right. Singing stops. Preacher looks around for the boys, but never indicates when he sees them. He sings happily as he gets down from the wagon. He carries a small jug and comes down center. He looks around and speaks in his best pulpit manner with double meaning for the boys).

The text today is: The Lord will deliver. Noah built the Ark and the animals went in, two by two. Then Noah looked about and said to the last two, "All is well. Get on board."

(Preacher kneels and pantomimes filling jug in the river. At the same time, Amos and Obie peek from left, then run quickly and hide in the cart. Preacher looks around cautiously, goes to cart, looks about once more, climbs onto cart, puts gunny-sacks over the

hidden boys. He snaps the reins, shouts, "Gette up," and the horse and cart move slowly to center. Singing starts with cart. Cue 5. "Who Built The Ark?" Preacher joggles the reins and bounces on the seat. After song, Preacher pulls on reins, frightened. Horse and cart stop at center. Boys peek out).

PREACHER. Whoa! Whoa! There's trouble up the road. Cover up. There's a man—with a gun!

(Boys quickly cover up. A white Man with a gun enters left).

MAN WITH GUN. Let's see your pass, boy. Where's your pass?

PREACHER. My pass?

MAN WITH GUN. Whose slave are you?

PREACHER. I ain't no slave, sir. I am a freedman. Got my papers right here.

(Takes paper from pocket and gives it to Man).

I travel around fixing pots and pans—and preaching a little.

MAN WITH GUN *(Gives paper back)*. I've heard about you. You're the tinker.

PREACHER. Yes, sir.

MAN WITH GUN. I'm stopping everybody on the road. I'm searching every wagon that comes this way.

PREACHER. What are you hunting?

MAN WITH GUN. I'm looking for a couple of little nigger boys that run away from Bricker's place.

PREACHER *(Innocently)*. Two runaways?

MAN WITH GUN. There's a reward out—twenty five bucks a head.

PREACHER *(Impressed)*. Twenty five dollars for each boy?

MAN WITH GUN. What you got in your wagon?

PREACHER. Pots and pans, some odds and ends.

MAN WITH GUN. What's in the barrel?

(Starts to barrel in which one boy is hiding).

PREACHER *(Loudly, starting his game of outwitting the guard)*. Was these two boys kind of ugly-looking?

MAN WITH GUN. All the notice said was twelve and ten years old.

(Puts his hand on barrel).

PREACHER *(Louder to get his attention)*. Did—did they have a fishing pole?

MAN WITH GUN. I reckon they did. They was last seen going fishing.

(Starts to lift cover).

What's in here?

PREACHER *(Shouts with joy).* Well, what do you know! That must of been them I saw!

MAN WITH GUN. Be who? Saw where?

PREACHER *(Taking his time).* There was a couple of boys that fit that description under the bridge this morning.

MAN WITH GUN. What bridge?

PREACHER. The new bridge over the Pee Dee River.

MAN WITH GUN. How long ago?

PREACHER. Oh, some hours.

MAN WITH GUN. They might still be there. All right, you can go on. Get along!

(He starts right).

PREACHER *(Happily).* Yes, sir!

MAN WITH GUN *(To himself).* I'll get there first.

PREACHER. Yes, sir.

MAN WITH GUN. And I'll get the reward.

(Exits right).

PREACHER *(Shouts in his victory).* NO-O-O-O-O, sir!

AMOS *(Boys pop up, eyes wide with fright).* He—he almost caught us.

OBIE. But you out-smarted him.

PREACHER. The Lord speaks in many tongues!

AMOS. They're hunting for us!

PREACHER *(Bitterly).* Men, hounds, and guns.

AMOS. What are we going to do?

PREACHER *(Also frightened).* We're getting out of here. Quick! I'm driving to Raleigh and start you on the underground railroad. Now—cover up and hold on tight. We're rolling on—to the Promised Land! Gette up!

(He slaps the reins. Boys hide. Singing starts. Cue 6. "The Old Ark's a-Moverin." Horse and cart move quickly off left, Preacher slapping the reins and bouncing on the seat. The lights dim to night. As the cart exits left, a wing flat is placed at right. The back flat is painted with shelves and bottles of a pharmacy. The flat at an angle on the left has a window with a practical curtain. A small counter-table is placed in the room. The singing dims and

stops. Mrs. Strauss enters right in the room. She is a sweet elderly lady, dressed in a robe and a night cap, and carries a lighted candle. Preacher enters at left, silently motions for the boys. Amos and Obie, frightened, follow him).

PREACHER *(Speaks cautiously)*. There is a light so they are still up. This is your first stop on the underground railroad. It's Mr. and Mrs. Strauss. He makes medicine. Now, quiet, and hide while I knock.

(Boys hide. Preacher looks around, then goes to room and knocks at an imaginary door. Mrs. Strauss pantomimes opening it).

MRS. STRAUSS. Why, it's Preacher Prentice. Come in.

PREACHER. Good evening, Mrs. Strauss. I've brought you two—

(Confidentially).

two—passengers.

MRS. STRAUSS. Passengers! Oh!

(Cautiously)

Keep watch outside. Don't let anyone see. And send in the two passengers.

(Preacher becomes a look-out, motions to boys who slip into the room. Mrs. Strauss closes the curtains at window. The boys huddle at one side, anxious and uncertain. Preacher enters and pantomimes closing the door).

MRS. STRAUSS. Why—they are children.

PREACHER. This is Amos and Obadiah. They are going on the underground to Philadelphia to their Pa.

MRS. STRAUSS. All alone? And so far!

PREACHER. Goodby, boys.

AMOS *(Afraid)*. Goodby, Preacher Prentice.

PREACHER. Remember, boys, keep going no matter what happens to you. Keep going on—to freedom.

OBIE. Goodby, Preacher Prentice. If you see Mama—

(Starts to cry).

Tell Mama—I miss her.

PREACHER. I'll tell her, Obie, and I'll also tell her how brave you are. God bless you all.

(He exits quickly at door, looks cautiously about and slips out at left).

MRS. STRAUSS *(Nervous)*. Mr. Strauss is sick. Upstairs. I'm sorry he can't help you.

Amos (*Frightened*). What are we going to do?

Mrs. Strauss. I know where he keeps the underground map. I will show you the next stop.

(*She puts small map on table*).

Make sure the curtains are closed. Nobody must see you.

(*Amos goes to window. She points to map*).

This is where you are—Raleigh, North Carolina.

Obie. Where is Phil—A—delph'a?

Mrs. Strauss. Up there.

Amos. It's not far at all!

Mrs. Strauss. It looks a small way on the map, but it is a long trip—beyond Richmond and Washington.

Obie. It's going to be a long walk, Amos.

Mrs. Strauss. You will get there, station by station. Your next stop is in Henderson at Doctor Culpepper's.

Amos. How far?

Mrs. Straus. Two days walking. You will hide in the woods at night and walk by day so you can read the names of the towns.

Amos. Read?

Mrs. Strauss. So you won't get lost.

Amos. We can't read.

Mrs. Strauss. Oh. And you can't *ask* anyone directions or they'll stop you. Well! We have a problem.

Amos. Yes, m'am.

Mrs. Strauss. But we will solve it.

Obie. How?

Mrs. Strauss. I will think. And I think better while I'm working. I'll put the covers out for you. You'll sleep here by the fire to-night.

(*Takes cover from counter and puts it on floor at right*).

Obie (*Frightened*). Amos, if we can't read signs, can't ask anybody, how are we going to find the way—to Phil—A—delph'a?

Amos. We got a problem.

Mrs. Strauss. I have the solution! But you will have to do some pretending.

Amos. Pretending?

Mrs. Strauss. You must make believe that you are Doctor Culpepper's slaves.

Amos. Yes, m'am. We can act like slaves real easy.

Mrs. Strauss. You will say that he sent you to get medicine from Mr. Strauss, and you're taking the medicine back to the doctor. I will write you a pass which you can show to anyone who stops you. Now I'll fix the medicine.

(Measures from jar on counter).

Pink pills, I think—and I will put "Poison" on the bottle. Would you like some?

(Offers them the big jar).

Amos *(Alarmed).* No, m'am. I ain't sick!

Mrs. Strauss *(Laughs).* Oh, it is not poison. It is not even medicine. It is candy.

Obie *(Eagerly).* Candy?

Mrs. Strauss *(Enjoying her joke).* You will be carrying a bottle of candy and no one will know the difference! Help yourself.

Obie. Yes, m'am.

(Boys eat candy hungrily).

Amos. Yes, M'am!

Mrs. Strauss. Now off to sleep. You must leave before sunup, slip away before anyone sees you.

Amos. Yes, m'am.

(Boys lie on cover. She tucks them in).

Mrs. Strauss. Many years ago I ran away. I ran away just like you, from my home in Europe. I wanted freedom too. People helped me. Now I can help you. Good night.

Amos. Goodnight. Thank you for the medicine.

Mrs. Strauss. So little . . . so young . . . running away to be free. Sleep well. And may your dream come true.

(Singing begins. Cue 7. "Steal Away". Mrs. Strauss writes note, quickly puts it by Amos, takes candle and exits right. Lights dim down. Scenery is moved off. Boys exit right. Lights come up and the singing changes to a lively beat. Cue 8. "Oh, a-Rock-a My Soul." Obie enters right. He suddenly points to the ground and starts to run after it. Amos enters right).

Obie. Look, Amos. There's a snake.

Amos. A snake? Let it be!

Obie. Lucky I didn't step on it.

Amos. Lucky it didn't bite you.

Obie. It's gone. It's free.

Amos. But we ain't. Not yet.

(Obie looks at him. Amos grins).

This morning we have to pretend we're slaves. How're you going to act, Obie, when the first white man stops you? Let's play-like you got the pass and you're going that way, and I'm coming this way with a gun.

(He gives Obie letter and then goes to center, turns and stops Obie. He comically overacts like the Man with the Gun).

Stop, boy, stop. Where's your pass?

Obie. Huh?

Amos. Where's your pass, boy?

Obie *(Grins and understands, then with great enjoyment over-acts the slave).* Oh, yes sir, yes, sir. I got a pass. Yes, sir.

Amos. Let's see it.

Obie. Yes, sir. Yes sir, here it is, sir.

Amos *(Pretends to read).* Doctor Culpepper—

(Grunts).

Obie. I think you are holding the letter upside down.

Amos. Don't get uppity with me, boy!

Obie. No, sir. No, sir!

Amos. You taking medicine back to your master?

Obie. Yes, sir. Yes, sir. Special medicine for liver trouble, belly trouble, and rhu—MI—tism.

Amos. Then go along, boy. Get along.

Obie. Yes, sir. Yes, sir.

(Passes Amos).

I'm getting along. Getting a long long way from here.

Amos *(Laughs and shouts).* And I'm getting along with you. Come on, Obie. We'll be at Henderson by tonight.

(Singing starts. Cue 9. "Gonna Sing All Along the Way." Boys run—free—in a circle several times around the stage. As they exit, a love seat and an ornate folding screen are placed on stage left, the screen is at the right of the sofa, making the corner of the room. Miss Melissa, a pretty young lady, beautifully dressed, enters left. She looks about nervously. She is high spirited, charm-

ing and affectionate. Singing dims out. She pantomimes closing the curtains at an imaginary window. She calls anxiously).

MELISSA. Come—come into the parlor. No one will see you here.

AMOS (*Amos and Obie slowly enter left, awed by the rich surroundings*). Is this Doctor Culpepper's house?

MELISSA. Yes. Papa is away on a sick call. Sit here.

(*Nervous, but gracious*).

Now, what can we do to entertain you?

OBIE. I like to sing!

MELISSA. Sh! No. Someone would hear us.

(*Looks about nervously*).

We'll read a story.

AMOS. We can't read.

MELISSA. I'll teach you! We'll play school.

(*Cautious again*).

Now sit and be very quiet while I get a book.

(*She exits left*).

AMOS (*Boys look about slowly*). Obie, we are in a parlor—a white folk's parlor—with a floor and a carpet.

OBIE. And lamps and curtains.

AMOS. And a sofa.

(*They both look at it*).

OBIE. Can we sit on it?

(*They look at it again and whisper*).

AMOS. Should we?

OBIE. Could we?

(*They nod to each other and run to sofa, then slowly sit down and smile with the feeling of comfort*).

AMOS. It's soft.

OBIE. It's bouncy.

(*They bounce gently, then faster and higher, and as the fun increases, they even start laughing*).

MELISSA (*Off*). No, Nellie. I won't need you any more. Good night.

(*Boys stop suddenly and stand with comic innocence. Melissa enters left with books*).

I found an old copybook. And for you, Obie——

OBIE. Yes, m'am?

MELISSA. I found a picture book of the Bible.

(Obie sits on floor with book. Amos sits on sofa with Melissa).

Now the first thing in reading is to learn the alphabet.

OBIE *(Points to picture in book)*. Look! They're whipping people with long whips.

MELISSA. Those are the Egyptians. They are whipping the Hebrew slaves.

OBIE. Are those slaves?

MELISSA. And that is Moses leading the slaves out of bondage.

(Doorbell rings loudly off left. Melissa is frightened and pulls the boys close to her).

Who can that be? Nellie, see who is at the door.

(Rises).

No. I had better go myself. Quick, boys, hide—hide and don't make a sound.

(Bell rings again and Melissa exits left. Boys look at each other. Obie points under the sofa. Amos shakes his head. They both look at screen, then nod, look off left. then tip-toe quickly to screen, each going behind it on either side).

MELISSA *(Off)*. Why, Edgar! How nice to see you—unexpectedly. Let me have your hat.

EDGAR *(Off)*. I couldn't wait until morning. I simply had to come and tell you.

(He strides into the room, bursting with excitement. He is a handsome young man, educated and a Southern gentleman. Melissa follows him, nervously looking for the boys).

It is the best of news, Melissa. It means that now we can set the date for the wedding.

MELISSA. Our wedding?

EDGAR. I am to be made a partner of the law firm. And that means a church wedding and everything you want.

MELISSA *(They embrace)*. Oh, Edgar.

EDGAR. Of course, it also means I will have to go to Philadelphia right away.

MELISSA. Philadelphia? Did you say Philadelphia, Edgar?

EDGAR. Yes. Oh, I feel badly, too. I don't want to be away from you either. But it will only be two months.

Melissa.   How will you go—to Philadelphia?

Edgar.   I'll drive, I suppose, in the carriage.

Melissa.   Edgar . . .?

Edgar.   What is it, Melissa?

Melissa.   Edgar, you do agree with Papa about the freeing of slaves?

Edgar.   Yes—but what has that to do with us?

Melissa.   I—I have something to tell you.

Edgar.   You sound so serious. What is it?

Melissa.   It is serious.

   (With determined effort).

I know the whereabouts of two runaway slaves.

Edgar.   What!

Melissa.   Two slaves are trying to get to Philadelphia. If they could go with you . . .?

Edgar *(Astounded).* You know the whereabouts of two runaway slaves? You are trying to help them!

Melissa.   Yes, Edgar.

Edgar.   Melissa, do you know what you are doing? What would your father say?

Melissa.   He has helped many slaves escape on the underground railroad.

Edgar.   Your father! But he's a born Southerner—a gentleman—a churchman. Melissa, does he know the penalties of slave-stealing?

Melissa.   Papa isn't a slave-stealer! He has freed his slaves.

Edgar.   The law says helping slaves to escape is the same as stealing them.

Melissa.   Papa thinks the law is unjust.

Edgar.   I agree. But one cannot disobey the law just because he doesn't agree with it.

Melissa.   What can you do then if the law tells you to do what you're sure is wrong?

Edgar.   Change the law! And I am certain that in fifty years slavery will be abolished.

Melissa.   Fifty years! What about the two little boys I am hiding now?

Edgar.   Hiding!

   (Looks around).

Melissa, we must turn these slaves over to the authorities at once! Where are they?

MELISSA. Authorities! Laws! That's all you know, Edgar.

EDGAR. You are in danger. You are risking your life.

MELISSA. If helping human beings is breaking the law, then I'm glad to risk my life, because I—I believe in the freedom of people.

EDGAR. This isn't like you, Melissa.

MELISSA. Yes, it is. You just don't know me. And I'm discovering that I don't know you.

EDGAR *(Incomprehensible)*. You—you are hiding slaves.

MELISSA. You had better go, Edgar.

EDGAR. Melissa, you must obey the law. Give up the slaves.

MELISSA. I must do what I think is right. Good night, Edgar.

EDGAR. Very well. I, too, must do what I think is right.

MELISSA. What do you mean?

EDGAR. I must report them. Good night, Melissa.

(Exits Left).

MELISSA *(Frightened)*. Edgar!

AMOS *(He and Obie peek around the screen and come out from either side)*. Is he gone?

MELISSA. Yes. And he is going to the authorities. We can't wait for Papa. I will take you to the next stop myself—tonight!

(Calls).

Nellie! Nellie, quick. Have John get the horses and carriage ready. Pack me a bag. I'm going to visit Cousin Emily. Hurry!

(To boys).

I will take you as far as South Hill. That is in Virginia. The next station is a tannery. It belongs to a Quaker named Elijah McNaul. There is a box at the back door for you to hide in. He checks it early every morning before the other men come to work, and he'll get you to the next station. Now sit there.

(Gives Obie his book).

And I'll be right back. We must hurry. Hurry before they find you!

(Exits left).

OBIE *(Amos looks after her, frightened. Obie points to picture in book quickly)*. Amos, look. Look at this picture again.

Amos. It's Moses leading the slaves out of bondage.

Obie. Yes. But look at the slaves. The slaves are white.

(They look at each other and then straight front in wonder. Singing starts. Cue 10. "Go Down Moses". The lights dim out. Boys exit left and sofa and screen are removed. A flat painted like the side of a building and with a large box attached to it is placed down center. Lights come up. It is night. Singing stops. Amos and Obie enter right, creeping quietly and looking around, frightened at the shadows).

Amos. Come on, Obie, come on.

Obie. It's so dark I can't see.

Amos. Take my hand.

Obie *(Noise is heard off right)*. What's that! What's that, Amos!

Amos. Quick! Hide—in the shadows.

(Boys separate and crouch and listen. An owl hoots).

Obie *(Terrified)*. Amos! Where are you?

Amos. It's just an owl. A hoot owl. Look! I think this is the tannery.

Obie. I'm tired, Amos. I can't go no farther.

Amos. It's the tannery! She said there was a box at the back.

(Comes down center).

There it is! We're here, Obie. It's all right. We can sleep in the box tonight.

(They look around, then slowly go to the box, whispering).

Don't make any noise when we raise the lid.

(Obie nods. They raise the lid slowly. Suddenly a figure springs up in the box and shouts).

Joe *(He is eighteen, another negro slave, bitter from bad treatment, and is aggressively hostile)*. Get out! Get out! You hear me! Get out of my box!

(Joe grabs Amos by the throat and starts choking and shaking him, still shouting, "Get out.").

Amos *(At the same time, yells)*. Stop! You're choking me. Stop! Stop!

(He screams frantic sounds as he tries to free himself).

Obie *(Hits at Joe and shouts)*. Let him loose! Let go! Let loose!

(Obie bites Joe's arm. Joe yells loudly and lets loose of Amos).

Amos! Amos! You all right, Amos?

Joe (*Looks at arm*). There's blood.

Amos (*To Obie*). What did you do, Obie?

Obie (*Facing front*). I bit him!

Joe. What you doing here?

Obie. Miss Melissa said to hide in the box.

Joe. You ain't going to hide in here. You ain't going to get in this box. It's mine. You hear me? Get going!

First Man (*Off left. He is gruff and straight-forward*). I didn't hear nothing.

Second Man (*He is mean and disagreeable. The two men enter left*). I heard something all right.

First Man (*Coming toward box*). Maybe a couple of tomcats meowing around.

Joe. Quick! Before they see you! Get in the box. Get in! Both of you! Hide!

(*Amos and Obie quickly climb into box. They close the lid just in time*).

First Man. Well, you can see—there's nobody around in the back.

(*Leans on box*).

Second Man. I heard scuffling and yelling.

First Man. You was dreaming.

(*Knocks his pipe on box*).

Second Man. It sounded like—like niggers talking.

First Man. Whatcha mean?

Second Man (*Pointedly*). Some folks think McNaul is hiding runaway slaves.

First Man. Hiding slaves?

Second Man. On the underground railroad.

(*Looks at side*).

I heard them all right. They was here.

First Man. The way you talk I might be standing right next to one —right now.

Second Man. They're hiding somewhere.

First Man. Naw. McNaul may be a little bible crazy, but he's not hiding runaway slaves. He ain't no criminal.

Second Man. He's a Quaker.

First Man. So what?

Second Man. He's different from us. And I don't trust him.

First Man. Come on. I'm going to bed.

(Exits left).

Second Man. I know I heard 'em. They was talking.

(Goes to left).

And I'm going to tell—tell the sheriff. He'll get 'em all right. He'll catch 'em. I'd like to catch one of them runaways myself.

(Second Man exits left. There is a pause. Then slowly the lid of the box is raised and six frightened eyes look about. First Joe stands up, then Amos, then Obie).

Joe. They're gone.

Obie. What if they'd opened the lid—and found us!

Joe. Now get going. I'm staying here and you're getting out. So get!

Amos. Go? We ain't got no place to go.

Obie. If we get out, we'll get caught.

Joe. Who cares if you do!

Obie *(Slowly and pointedly)*. If we get caught—first thing they'll ask us is—do we know of any other runaway slaves? And I do. You. And I always tell the truth.

Amos. We got to stay. We got to hide here.

Joe *(Grudgingly)*. I reckon you do.

Amos. My name is Amos. My brother's name is Obadiah.

Obie. What's your name?

Joe *(Angrily)*. Joe.

Obie. Move over, Joe. You're taking more than your share.

Amos *(Anxiously)*. We ought to put the lid down and hide.

(He sits down in box, out of sight).

Obie. And go to sleep.

(Joe slinks down out of sight. Obie clasps his hands in prayer).

Thank you Lord for helping us this far and please help us some more tomorrow. Bless Mama and Pa and Sally and Amos. Amen.

(He disappears but re-appears at once).

And bless Preacher Prentice and Mrs. Strauss and Miss Melissa. Amen.

(He disappears but re-appears at once).

And—and bless Joe. Amen.

(Joe rises up and pushes Obie down out of sight. Joe quietly lets the lid down. There is silence. The lights slowly come up to morning brightness. Elijah McNaul strides in from right. He is a large powerful man who voices his strong convictions. He goes to box, looks around, then lifts the lid slowly).

McNaul. Good morning. Welcome, pilgrims. Welcome to my tannery.

Amos *(Boys stand up cautiously)*. Are you—Master McNaul who is going to help us?

McNaul. I am Elijah McNaul. Not master. No one is a master to thee. Never let me hear thee call any man master.

Amos. Yes, sir, Master McNaul.

Obie. Yes, Mister McNaul.

McNaul *(Points at Obie)*. Thee—has some stuffing in thy head. Come. Out of the box and go inside. Thee must eat quickly before the men come to work.

(Boys climb out of box. McNaul points and boys go single file around the right of flat and out of sight behind it).

Then thee will climb up to the loft and hide there until it is night.

(Looks up).

So beginneth another day which the Lord hath made.

(Singing begins. Cue 11. "Heav'n Bound Soldier." McNaul exits right behind flat. The flat is turned around. The other side is painted like the top of a loft. McNaul enters from behind flat from left, followed by Amos, Obie and Joe. Singing stops).

McNaul. Now up the ladder to the loft.

(He sets up an imaginary ladder. Amos looks up, then pantomimes climbing the ladder).

Thee will stay up there until I call thee tonight.

(Joe pantomimes climbing ladder).

Running . . . hiding . . . like frightened sparrows.

(Obie pantomimes climbing ladder).

No man can own another man. It is blasphemy!

(Boys stand center, frightened at his voice).

Close the trap door!

(Amos pantomimes closing door).

Take care. Do not walk or talk or make a sound. The men below will hear thee. And remember and let it be a comfort—God has his eye on the smallest sparrow.

(Pantomimes taking down the ladder and carrying it off, as he exits left).

OBIE.   He talks like the Bible.

AMOS *(Sits down).* Miss Melissa said he is a Quaker.

JOE.   He's white. I don't trust no white folks.

OBIE.   Joe—what did you do to your face?

(Points at long scar running from Joe's eye to his lower jaw).

JOE.   I didn't do nothing.

(Turns away hiding scar).

OBIE.   There's a big scar.

JOE.   Master did it—with a whip. Cut my face open.

OBIE.   He must be a wicked man.

JOE.   He's a devil. All the whites are devils.

OBIE.   Master Bricker wasn't a devil. He was stingy but he never whipped us.

AMOS.   But he could of. He owned us—and that ain't right.

OBIE.   He was born a slave owner, just like we was born slaves.

JOE.   I wasn't born a slave.

OBIE.   Where was you born?

JOE.   In Africa.

AMOS.   Africa?

JOE *(Slowly and proudly).* I was born in Africa.

(To Obie).

Now don't ask me why I left. I didn't have no choice.

OBIE.   Why did you leave, Joe?

JOE *(Pause. Then he relives the bitter memory).* I was little—maybe four or five. They come to our village. They caught my mother and the baby and caught me. White folks chained us on a boat. Hid us down below so nobody could see us. It was dark and it stunk and the baby cried all the time 'cause my mother couldn't feed him and then after a time he stopped crying—and he was dead. Lots of people was dead. And then my mother died and the white folks took her away—

(Suddenly turns on Obie).

What'd you ask me that for! Leave me be! Leave me be!

AMOS *(Quietly).* We ought to go to sleep.

(He and Obie lie down together).

JOE (*Sits alone*). I've been running—running for three days. Running
—running—running—

(*Drops his head exhausted*).

McNAUL (*He hurries in at left, quickly pantomimes putting up the
ladder to trap door, and calls excitedly*). Boys! Boys! Hear me,
boys!

(*Boys are immediately at trap door. They speak together as Mc-
Naul continues*).

Get thee to the trap door! Open it, boys. Quick!

AMOS. It's Mister McNaul.

OBIE. Something's wrong.

McNAUL. Down! Down the ladder. It is not safe here.

(*Obie pantomimes climbing down*).

Someone reported thee. Quick! Slave catchers are coming. They
will find and catch thee.

(*Amos pantomimes climbing down*).

Run through the back to the river. Swim! Follow the river to
Petersburg.

(*Joe pantomimes climbing down*).

Go to Miss Holkum's house behind the bank. There are two horseshoes above the door.

(*Boys run off left*).

Run, boys, run. Run for your life!

(*Singing begins. Cue 12. "You'd Better Run," followed by spoken
and clapped rhythms. McNaul exits upper left. Flat is removed
off upper left. Singing increases in tempo. Joe runs across from
left to right*).

JOE (*Calls and motions to boys*). Run—run!

(*Joe exits right. Amos, followed by Obie, runs across from left
to right*).

AMOS. Run, Obie. Run!

OBIE (*Stumbles. Amos quickly helps him*). My foot.

AMOS. I'll help you.

(*A red glow of light is seen upper left*).

OBIE. Look! A fire!

AMOS. It's the tannery.

OBIE. It's on fire!

Amos. They're burning the loft. They're burning us!

Joe *(Runs in at right and motions)*. Run—run!

(The stage is now red as the flames leap higher. Amos and Obie run, repeating in terror).

Amos. Run—run—run—

Obie. Run—run—run—

Joe *(Follows them)*. Run—run—run—

(They exit right as singing builds to a climax. The curtains close.

NOTE. There may be a short intermission or the play may be continued, with the curtains opening immediately on the next scene).

ACT TWO

(Singing is heard. Cue 13. "Steal Away." The curtains open on a bare stage. Amos enters from left. He is tired and frightened. He comes to footlights and speaks).

Amos. We ran and we hid and we got to Petersburg. We found Miss Holkum's house with the horseshoes above the door, but they didn't bring good luck to us. She had a sickness and it was catching. She told us how to get on to Richmond and we slept there one night at Reverend Pringle's. Then we started stealing our way to Hanover, the next station.

(Moves to left).

We were walking along the road that night close to a stone fence,

(A section of a stone fence is placed center, at an angle. Lights dim to night).

and we came to a couple of farm houses. The dogs heard us and they started barking, waking everybody up.

(Loud dog barks are heard off. Joe runs in down left, followed by Obie. Amos joins them).

Joe. Come on! Before the dogs catch us!

Amos *(Points left)*. Someone's on the porch. He's got a gun!

Joe. Hide—hide by the fence!

(Boys run to fence, crouch and hide. Jud, a farmer, enters left with shot gun).

Who is it? Who's there? I heard you. Whatcha doing prowling around my house? Where are you?

Joe. Over the fence and run for it!

(Boys scramble over the fence).

Jud. Stop! Stop or I'll shoot.

(*He fires the gun three times in the direction of fence. Boys, at right, fall to the ground for cover and remain motionless. Jud cautiously comes to fence*).

I seen you. You won't get away. I gotcha covered and I'll shoot you if you move—shoot you dead.

(*Jud starts to climb wall, slips and falls, firing the gun. There is a loud gun report. He crumbles in pain and moans loudly, sits up rubbing his leg*).

Oh! Oh, my leg!

Amos (*Amos raises his head and looks about. Then Joe does. Then Obie*). You all right, Obie?

Obie. He didn't shoot me.

(*Jud moans louder*).

What happened to him?

Joe (*Looks cautiously*). I think—he shot hisself.

Jud. My leg. My leg.

Joe (*Boys look toward wall, then cautiously cross to the back of it. They peek over, Jud moans and rubs his leg*). He's hurt. Now's our chance to get away. Run!

(*Joe and Amos exit right, but Obie leans over the wall*).

Obie. You—you all right, Mister?

Jud. The gun went off when I was getting over the fence. Must have shot my leg.

Joe (*Joe and Amos enter right*). Come on. Come on!

Jud. Get help from the next house. You can't leave me here to die.

Joe. Get help? You crazy! You was shooting at us. You was going to kill us.

(*Grabs Obie*).

Come on!

Obie. He'll die.

Joe. They ain't going to catch me just 'cause of you. Come on!

(*Joe pulling Obie, exits right*).

Jud. Wait. Fetch my neighbor. I'll bleed to death.

Amos (*Looks at left where Jud points at neighbor's house, then calls off right*).

You go on. I'll catch up with you.

(He quickly turns and runs back to extreme left, knocks at an imaginary door. He knocks again. First Neighbor enters at left).

FIRST NEIGHBOR. What you knocking for? What you want?

AMOS. Please, sir, your neighbor, he's hurt real bad—over by the fence.

FIRST NEIGHBOR *(Grabs Amos by shoulder).* Who are you?

SECOND NEIGHBOR *(Enters from left).* What's going on?

FIRST NEIGHBOR. He says Jud's hurt. Must of been the shots we heard.

SECOND NEIGHBOR. Where is he?

AMOS. By the fence. Now let me go.

(He struggles).

FIRST NEIGHBOR. Oh no. We're going to keep you. Get a rope. Tie him up.

(Second Neighbor exits left).

AMOS. Please let me go. I told you where he was.

FIRST NEIGHBOR. What are you? A runaway? We'll find out to-morrow.

(Second Neighbor enters left with rope and ties Amos' hands behind him).

That will hold you tonight and teach you a lesson. You won't be running away now. Where is Jud?

AMOS. By the fence.

FIRST NEIGHBOR *(Goes to fence. Jud moans).* Jud—is that you?

JUD. Oh! Thank God you've come.

(First Neighbor helps Jud up. Second Neighbor holds Amos).

FIRST NEIGHBOR. What happened?

JUD. The gun went off—accidentally—shot my leg.

FIRST NEIGHBOR. Easy. Easy. I'll help you to the house.

(He helps Jud. They go left).

JUD. Get the doctor from town.

SECOND NEIGHBOR *(Pushes Amos).* What about him?

FIRST NEIGHBOR. Put him in the shed. There may be a reward. Lock him up.

(First Neighbor exits with Jud).

SECOND NEIGHBOR *(Pulls Amos down left, then pantomimes opening a door).* Get in the shed.

(Pushes Amos through the imaginary door).

You won't steal away again. We'll lock you up till tomorrow. Then you know what will happen, don't you? You know what they'll do to a runaway slave?

(He pantomimes shutting the door, putting a peg in the latch, and exits left).

AMOS *(His courage and hopes are gone. He speaks softly and sadly).* I had to help him, Mama. He was hurt. And now—I'm caught. They'll beat me. Sell me to another master.

(Starts to cry).

I tried, Mama. I tried to get to Pa.

(Crying freely).

But—but Obie will make it.

(Trying to stop crying).

Please, please let Obie get away—and be free.

(Buries his head, shaking with sobs).

I tried, Mama. I tried.

(His sobs become quieter. Obie enters left, stops, frightened but determined, looks around carefully, and moving cautiously comes to center).

OBIE *(Calls softly).* Amos . . .? Amos . . .?

(Amos slowly raises his head).

Amos . . .?

AMOS. Is that you, Obie?

OBIE. Yes. Are you in the shed?

AMOS. Yes.

OBIE. You got to get out. Quick. It's almost light.

AMOS. I can't. I'm tied up and the door's locked.

OBIE. Maybe there's a loose board. I'll feel.

(He pantomimes feeling carefully around the shed).

If I had a shovel, I could dig you out.

AMOS. There's no way out. I'm caught. But you can still get away. You go on—go on with Joe.

OBIE. Leave you?

AMOS. Go on Obie! If you stay, they'll catch you, too.

OBIE. I ain't going to leave you, Amos! I'll find a way. I'll get you out!

Amos.   Go on, Obie. And keep on going—Pa's waiting for you.

Obie.   He's waiting for both of us!

(He is at the imaginary door and is elated).

Amos—Amos! The door—it isn't locked! It's just a wooden peg.
I can pull it out!

*(Pantomimes pulling peg out and opens door and goes to Amos.
He speaks with relief, love, and joy).*

Oh, Amos.

Amos *(Answers with the same sincere emotion).* Obie.

(As Obie unties him).

Where's Joe?

Obie.   On ahead. We hid. We saw them tie you up. We thought sure
you was a goner.

Amos.   So did I.

Obie.   Joe tried to pull me away, but I couldn't leave you, Amos.

Amos.   How did you get rid of him?

Obie *(Proudly).* I—bit him.

Amos *(Freed of ropes, stretches).* We'll catch up with him at the next
stop, at Bowling Green.

Obie.   Come on.

(They slip out the door and creep silently left). It's getting light.

Amos.   There's just one star left.

Obie.   Amos, do you know what I think? I think maybe—there's a
good angel watching and looking out for us.

*(Singing begins. Cue 14. "The Angel Of The Lord". Obie holds
out his hand. Amos takes it. They exit slowly at left. Fence is
removed. Lights come up to morning. Singing stops. Loud shouts
and repeated gun shots are heard upper left. "There he goes . . .
get him . . . he's heading for the house . . . etc." Joe runs in upper
left, terrified and desperate, looks back; there is more shouting.
He runs down left. The way is blocked. He turns, rushes to right.
He is suddenly met by Old Man, who enters right, shot gun pointed
at Joe. Joe stops).*

Old Man.   Stop. You ain't running no place, boy.

Young Man *(Enters upper left).* You get him?

Old Man.   I got him. Tie his hands.

(Young Man ties Joe's hands).

We'll take him into town. He's a real husky one. Ought to be worth a big reward.

YOUNG MAN. They say there are three of them.

OLD MAN. Three?

YOUNG MAN. They say they shot a farmer down the road.

OLD MAN. A real mean one, huh? Shooting white folks. You got to learn your place boy. And I reckon you will when your master gets you back. He'll take it right out of your hide.

(Gives gun to Young Man).

Keep him covered. We'll take him to town.

(Young Man puts gun at Joe's back and guides him off right. Old Man follows).

Step lively, boy. No more running for you. You're caught.

(They exit).

OBIE *(He and Amos crawl in down left. They are frightened).* Did they catch Joe?

AMOS. Yes. Tied him up and they're taking him away.

(Off right, there are excited shouts and several gun shots. "Look out . . . He got away . . . Get him! etc." Joe runs in from right. There are more gun shots. Joe is hit in the back. He staggers and falls. Amos and Obie hide by flattening themselves on the ground. The two men run in right).

OLD MAN. Why did you shoot? What did you shoot him for? You stupid idiot!

(Old Man kneels over Joe).

He's dead. You think his master's going to pay us for a dead slave? You dumb blundering fool! Well, pick him up! We'll get rid of him.

(They drag Joe off right).

There are two more. We'll get the other two. They can't be far. We'll get them—alive.

(They exit right).

OBIE *(Amos, then Obie, slowly rise up).* What happened?

AMOS. Don't look, Obie. Don't look.

(Holds Obie close so he can't see).

OBIE. Did they get Joe?

AMOS. Joe's dead.

OBIE. But he was just alive. I saw him running.

Amos. He's dead. They shot him. Now they'll hunt us! We're next, Obie. We got to get to Bowling Green—before they get us! Come on! Run! Run!

Obie (*Nods. Singing starts. Cue 15. "You'd Better Run"*). Run!

Amos. Run for your life!

(They exit left. A small kitchen table and a stool are placed down right. Jack Johnson, a free negro, good natured and unafraid, enters right and sits at table reading a book. Lights come up on room area at right. "Run" rhythms stop. Jack turns a page and yawns. Amos and Obie slip in from left, very cautiously. They hide, venture again, as they cross to right. Amos pantomimes peeking in an imaginary window, then motions Obie to follow, and they silently go to left side of room and pantomime knocking softly at a door. Jack raises his head. Amos knocks a second time. Jack goes to and pantomimes opening the door. He looks at the weary and frightened boys).

Jack. Come in.

(Boys enter room).

I was waiting up for you. You're kind of late getting to Bowling Green.

Amos. How did you know we'd come?

Jack. I heard about you. But they said there were three of you.

Amos. There was. But Joe—they shot Joe.

Obie. He's dead.

Jack. Sit down.

(Obie sits wearily and rests his head on the table).

The sheriff was here tonight—looking for you.

Amos. How'd he know to come here?

Jack. Some of my good neighbors complained that I have too many night visitors.

(Innocently).

They think I'm part of the underground railroad.

(Laughs).

But they haven't caught me yet—and they ain't going to. Sheriff said you shot a white man.

Amos. He shot hisself.

Jack. Well, they're out looking for you. And we've got to move you on fast. It ain't safe for you here. But how am I going to get the two of you out of town? They'll be combing the country for two runaway boys.

(Boys look at each other frightened).

It's most day light and I'll have to go to work as usual.

(Thinking aloud).

Now—I could take the little one with me. I sometimes take my own little boy along while I chop wood. But that leaves you.

OBIE. I ain't going to leave Amos!

JACK. Hush! You'll wake up the family.

(Nods to right. He looks at Amos).

My other one is a girl. About your size.

AMOS. I ain't a girl.

JACK. 'Course you ain't, and they're not looking for a girl—are they?

(Beams with an idea).

That's it!

AMOS. What's it?

JACK. You wait. I'll be right back—with a dress.

(He exits right).

OBIE. What's he thinking?

AMOS. I don't know, but I hope it's not what I think he's thinking.

JACK *(Enters right, holding out a dress and bandana).* You—will be my—little girl.

AMOS. Me?

JACK. Now put on this dress.

AMOS. Me!

JACK. Put this bandana over your head. Make yourself real pretty.

(Give Amos bandana and dress).

Now I'll get my axe and you and me—

(To Obie).

we'll go to the woods. We'll walk down the road, singing—like I do every morning.

(To Amos).

Then you come along—all pretty-like in a dress—with my lunch pail. If anybody stops you, you say—real sweet-like—you're taking your Pa his lunch which he forgot. Then follow the road in the woods. You'll hear me chopping and singing.

AMOS. I don't want to be—a girl!

Jack. What's wrong? You scared?

Amos. Huh?

Jack. I figure this will be the bravest thing you've ever done, and— you have to do it all by yourself. You big enough to do it?

(Amos nods).

And tonight I'll start you on the cattle path to Fredericksburg. The next station is at the Webber farm.

(To Obie).

Come on—

(Pointedly).

son. Can you sing?

(Obie nods).

Then sing. Helps keep up your courage—and the white folks, they like to see us happy.

(Jack and Obie pantomime exiting at door and exit off left. Amos looks at dress. Then like taking bitter medicine, he braces himself, quickly puts it over his head and masculinely strides around the table. He puts bandana on his head, picks up lunch pail and sits, pulling up his skirt and crossing his legs. Singing begins. Cue 16. "Jim Crack Corn." Lights dim out on room area. Amos exits right, as furniture is taken off. Jack and Obie enter left and cross. Singing dims out as Jack and Obie sing the same song with forced cheerfulness. They see a Patrol with gun who enters right. They stop singing, look at each other, then start singing louder).

Jack. Morning.

Patrol. Morning.

(Jack and Obie pass the Patrol, look at each other, smile, then start singing).

Just a minute.

(Jack and Obie stop).

You see anyone up the road?

Jack. No, sir. You looking for someone?

Patrol. We got a patrol out for two runaway slave boys.

Jack. Two runaway boys?

Patrol. They say they're dangerous.

Jack. Goodness me! What kind of dangerous?

Patrol. Shot a farmer. There's a reward for them.

Jack. Well, what do you know!

Patrol. Keep a look out.

Jack. Yes, sir!

Patrol. They won't get by me.

Jack. No, sir! Come along—son.

(Takes Obie's hand).

No, sir, they sure won't get by you.

(Jack and Obie look at each other and start singing and exit right. Patrol follows them to right. Amos enters left, sees Patrol and stops frightened. Summing up his courage, he walks toward Patrol. He stops, remembering he is a girl, he takes smaller steps).

Patrol *(Turns and sees him).* Where are you goin'?

Amos. 'Cuse me, sir—

(Raises his voice).

'cuse me, sir.

Patrol. Yes? Speak up.

Amos. Did you see my Papa?

Patrol. Your Papa?

Amos. And my brother go by this way?

Patrol. He a woodcutter?

Amos. Yes, sir.

(Raises voice).

Yes, sir.

Patrol. They went down the road.

(Smiles).

You his little girl?

Amos. Yes, sir.

(Raises voice).

Yes, sir.

Patrol *(Pleasantly).* And I must say you're a mighty pretty little girl.

(Amos comically smiles back at him).

You taking his lunch to him?

(Amos nods).

That's a nice little girl. Go along, now. Go along to your Papa. I'm patroling the road. Two runaways going north, but they're not going to get past me.

AMOS. No, sir. No, sir. They won't get past you.

(Pass Patrol).

PATROL. Now run along.

AMOS. Yes, sir. I'll run. I'll run. I'll run!

(Amos runs off right. Patrol exits left. Singing begins. Cue 17. "Oh, a-Rock-a My Soul." Lights come up bright. Obie enters left, running happily, pulling a small kite which is on a short string. He circles and skips and laughs. One of his bare feet has a bandage on it. A plain bench is placed down left. A box-trunk is put at left. Will Webber enters left. He is fifteen, a wholesome and manly young boy. He carries a book. Singing stops).

OBIE. Look, Will. It flies like a bird.

(He stops, out of breath, comes to bench where Will sits).

It's nice here on your farm. Sitting on the back porch and knowing today I'll have fried chicken again with potatoes—all I can eat—and I'll be sitting right at the table with white folks.

WILL. I'm glad thee is here. And mother says thee and Amos must stay in Fredericksburg. Stay here with us on the farm until your foot is well and thee are rested before you go on.

(Amos enters down left, in boys clothes).

OBIE. Look, Amos. Watch! It flies like a bird—in the sky—

(He circles with kite).

Whee-ee-ee! I'm a bird. I can fly—in the sky.

(He exits right).

AMOS. Obie never had no playthings before.

WILL. I brought a new book for us to read. Thee is learning to read very quickly.

AMOS. What did you write on the first page?

WILL *(Smiles and reads proudly).* I wrote: Will Webber is my name. Fredericksburg is my location. Heaven is my destination. You can write that in your first book. "Amos is my name—" But thee should have a last name.

AMOS. I never had one. But Pa—in his letter said he'd taken the name of—Carpenter.

WILL *(Stands and they shake hands).* Amos Carpenter.

AMOS. How many more miles is it to Philadelphia?

WILL. About two hundred.

AMOS. We should be starting.

WILL. Mother says thee are not to walk any further.

AMOS. How we going to get there?

WILL. I said—if *I* could go to Philadelphia and visit Grandfather, I could take the train and take Obie and thee with me.

AMOS. Could you?

WILL. No. Mother said it would look very strange for a Quaker boy to have two negro servants. And that the train stations are watched, you know, very closely by slave-catchers.

AMOS. We got to get to Pa some how.

WILL. I wish I could help you. Oh, I wish I could put thee both in my pocket.

(Looks at trunk and smiles with a new idea).

And I can!

AMOS. How?

WILL. I can put thee in my luggage.

AMOS. Luggage?

WILL. I can put thee in the trunk!

(Points to trunk).

You can ride on the train all the way to Philadelphia—inside the trunk and nobody will know! Obie! Come here, and see if thee will fit!

(They pull trunk forward excitedly and raise lid).

Get in. Try it out for size.

(Amos steps into trunk).

Mother can put padding around the corners. We can make air holes so thee can breathe.

AMOS *(Holds nose, raises one hand as if he is jumping into water).* One, two, three.

(He disappears in trunk).

WILL *(Obie runs in from right).* Here, Obie, get thee in the trunk.

AMOS *(Head appears).* With me.

(Head disappears).

OBIE *(Climbs into trunk).* What are we playing? What is the name of the game?

AMOS *(Stands up by Obie).* Philadelphia is—my destination!

(Amos and Obie disappear and Will closes the lid on the trunk. Singing begins. Cue 18. "Git On Board." Mother enters down

left, and stands with back toward audience. She holds a cap and coat for Will who puts them on. Then he speaks over low humming).

WILL. Goodby, Mother. Don't worry. I won't lose my ticket and Grandfather will meet us. Goodby. I'll take good care of the trunk—and everything that is in it. Don't cry, Mother. I know it is a dangerous trip, but I'll be careful. Goodby. Goodby.

(Two stagehands enter upper left and carry trunk to center. Mother waves and backs off down left. Will waves, then turns to trunk as stagehands set it down with a loud bang. Singing stops).

Please—please be careful! There are—breakable things inside the trunk.

(Stagehands exit upper right).

CONDUCTOR *(Calls and enters down right).* All aboard. All aboard for Washington, Baltimore, Philadelphia, New York.

WILL. Mister, mister, can I ride in the baggage car with my trunk?

CONDUCTOR *(Crosses to left).* Don't make no difference to me where you ride, sonny, just as long as you pay your fare.

WILL. Oh, I have my ticket—to Philadelphia.

(Gives him ticket).

CONDUCTOR. All aboard! All aboard!

(Conductor exits left. Singing starts slowly then gains in speed as the train moves. Cue 19. "Train Song").

WILL *(Stands by trunk and smiles, eyes following the passing scenery from left to right).* We're moving. We're on our way.

(Knocks on top of trunk. There is an answering knock inside).

Thee will soon be free.

(Singing swells, then dims as Will cautiously lifts lid of trunk and Amos and Obie peek out).

AMOS. Look, Obie, through the crack in the door. See the trees go by.

(Their eyes move with the passing scenery).

OBIE. So fast.

WILL. Grandfather wrote he would contact your father.

AMOS. Pa?

WILL. And tell him I am bringing two special pieces of luggage. Thee must be careful even in Pennsylvania because of the Fugitive Slave Law.

CONDUCTOR *(Enters left).* Hey there, sonny.

(Lid closes quickly).

Who are you talking to?

WILL.   Talking to?

(Sits on trunk).

CONDUCTOR.   There's no live-stock in the trunk, is there? Let's see.

WILL.   No, sir. No, sir. I—I was just—talking to myself.

CONDUCTOR *(Crosses).* Oh, well, I talk to myself, too. I figure I have a better conversation with myself than when I talk to some people. We're coming into Washington.

(Exits right).

WILL.   Washington!

(Knocks on trunk).

We've come as far as Washington.

AMOS *(Trunk lid raises. Amos and Obie nod, smile and repeat).* Washington.

(Lid is lowered. Will sits on trunk with arms folded. Singing swells and then dims).

CONDUCTOR *(Off, calls).* Baltimore. Baltimore. All aboard!

(Singing swells and then dims. Will stands and knocks on trunk. Lid is lifted and Amos and Obie peek out).

WILL.   We just crossed a big river and I think it was the Susquehanna, so that means we're in Pennsylvania.

CONDUCTOR *(Off right, calls).* Philadelphia! Next stop—Philadelphia.

(Trunk lid closes quickly as Conductor enters).

This is your station, sonny. Philadelphia.

(He exits left).

WILL.   Yes, sir. Thank you, sir.

(Singing swells and then stops. Two stagehands enter left).

Please, will you take my trunk to my Grandfather's house. This is the address.

(He gives them a piece of paper).

And please, please, handle the trunk—carefully. It contains two precious—gifts.

(Stage hands put trunk down at right and exit).

Amos . . . Obie . . . we are here. Thee can lift the lid. Thee has come—to your free home.

(Will beckons off right. Pa, wonderfully real, enters down right, and stands at side. Will exits right. Amos and Obie raise the lid slowly, stand and smile to each other. They step out of the trunk, look at the free ground they are standing on, look around, then breathe deeply).

PA *(Steps forward).* Amos?

(Another step).

Obadiah?

AMOS *(Boys look at him, at each other and then back at him).* Pa?

OBIE. Pa?

PA. My boys!

(Holds out his arms).

AMOS *(Both boys run to him, shouting).* Pa! Pa!

(They embrace).

We're here, Pa. We're here.

OBIE. We made it!

PA. My two big boys! Let me look at you. And you come all the way from South Carolina—by yourselves!

AMOS *(Proudly).* Five hundred miles.

OBIE. On the underground railroad!

PA. How did you do it? How did you do it!

AMOS. I think Obie said it right. It was like there was a good angel —and good people—watching over us.

(Choir starts to hum. Cue 20. "Steal Away." Preacher enters from left and crosses to right and stands).

First there was Preacher Prentice who brought your letter and started us on the way.

(Mrs. Strauss enters right, crosses left, stands by Preacher).

And then Mrs. Strauss who fixed candy medicine and wrote us a pass.

(Melissa enters right, crosses, stands by Mrs. Strauss).

And Miss Melissa who drove us in her carriage to Virginia.

(McNaul enters right, stands by Melissa).

And Mister McNaul who hid us in the loft—with Joe.

(Jack enters right and stands by McNaul).

And Reverend Pringle in Richmond and Jack who helped us and dressed me up like a girl.

(Mother and Will enter right and stand by Jack).

And last, Mrs. Webber on the farm and Will who hid us in his trunk and all by himself brought us—home. Together—from one to the next, to the next—

(Actors across the back in a semi-circle, one by one join hands).

they helped us—all the way. And now when we get Mama—

(Mama enters down left and stands by Pa and Obie).

and Sally—we'll all be together—free.

(Choir sings softly, "Steal Away." Amos comes to footlights and stands at center. Singing stops. Proudly and joyfully he announces).

My name is Amos Carpenter.
On free land is my location.
And—

(Smiles happily).

Heaven is my destination.

(Singing begins. Cue 21. "Didn't My Lord Deliver Daniel?" The rest of the cast enters from left, cross to right and stand behind the principals. All sing with spirit and clap in rhythm).

The End